W9-CBU-179

# SPECIAL INTERESTS

FROM

## LOBBYISTS

*to*

SANDY DONOVAN

LERNER PUBLICATIONS ◆ MINNEAPOLIS

Lerner Publications Company
A division of Lerner Publishing Group, Inc.
241 First Avenue North
Minneapolis, MN 55401 USA

For reading levels and more information, look up this title at www.lernerbooks.com.

Main body text set in Calvert MT Std Light 10/16.
Typeface provided by Monotype Typography.

**Library of Congress Cataloging-in-Publication Data**

Donovan, Sandra, 1967–
    Special interests : from lobbyists to campaign funding / by Sandy Donovan.
        pages cm. — (Inside elections)
    Includes bibliographical references.
    ISBN 978-1-4677-7912-8 (lb : alk. paper) — ISBN 978-1-4677-8523-5 (pb : alk. paper) — ISBN 978-1-4677-8524-2 (eb pdf)
    1. Pressure groups—Juvenile literature. 2. Lobbying—Juvenile literature. 3. Campaign funds—Juvenile literature. I. Title.
JF529.D66 2016
622.4'30973—dc23                                    2014041405

Manufactured in the United States of America
1 – VP – 7/15/15

# CONTENTS

# The BIG MONEY of POLITICS

I magine you're checking out the news during breakfast. A few prominent storylines catch your eye as they roll down the screen:

"Interest groups barrage Congress"

"Lobbyists schmooze at lavish convention parties"

"'Fixing' campaign finance is only making it worse"

Interest groups, lobbyists, and campaign finance reform— if these topics are all over the news, it's probably an election year. Maybe you know what some of these terms mean. Or maybe you prefer to toss on your headphones and crank up your favorite music whenever the topics come up.

These buzzwords may sound confusing or boring to you. But the people and the groups behind these words have a huge impact on the political system in the United States. Billions of dollars flow through interest groups and political campaigns each year. And that money can have a huge influence on laws and policies that affect you, your friends, your family, and all the other citizens in the country.

Barack Obama's 2012 presidential campaign raised $1.123 billion. That total doesn't even include money gathered by special interest groups that supported his reelection.

Interest groups, lobbyists, and campaign funding can affect elections in a big way. These factors are at the very core of the election process in the United States. They each have good qualities and not-so-good qualities. But they definitely make a big difference in who ends up in office—whether it's a mayor's office, a congressional office, or the White House's Oval Office. Once you understand what these words and phrases mean, you can analyze the news stories yourself and form your own opinions about what you learn. That's a key part of your job as a citizen in a democracy.

# CHAPTER ONE

# The SKYROCKETING COSTS of ELECTIONS

**H**ave you ever noticed that people love to argue about elections, elected people, and just about anything else having to do with politics? It sometimes seems as though people on both sides of the political aisle—meaning Democrats on one side and Republicans on the other—have agreed to *never* agree on anything. And then there are those outside the two main parties, who agree on some issues and disagree on others.

There's one fact that nobody can disagree with: elections are expensive—superexpensive. And they're getting more expensive every year.

## WHY DO ELECTIONS COST SO MUCH?

Most of the money spent on elections goes toward marketing. Think about the goal of an election: each candidate is trying to convince voters that she or he is the best person for whatever position they're all running for. Think about all the marketing actions you might take to convince anywhere from a few thousand voters (for a local election) to a few hundred

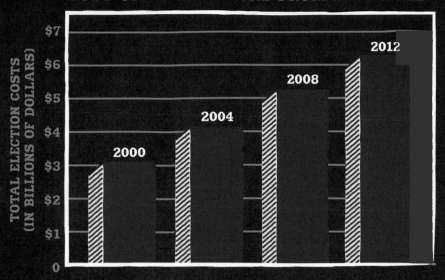

## COST OF US ELECTIONS FROM 2000–2012

National elections are the most expensive in the country—and the costs go up with each subsequent election. From 2000 to 2012, total cost of the US presidential and congressional elections more than doubled—from about $3.1 billion to nearly $6.3 billion per election. When all the numbers are added up, the 2016 presidential election is expected to be the most expensive in history.

million voters (for a national election) that they should vote for you. Below is a short list of activities—expensive activities—candidates spend money on:

1. **Figure out the best way to persuade people to elect you.** For most candidates, this means hiring several political consultants to study the issues and how people react to them. Political consultants aren't cheap. They sometimes charge hundreds of dollars per hour for their services.

2. **Give speeches and talk to as many voters, in person, as you possibly can.** This is the way you spread the

news about what a great candidate you are. This also means you'll have travel expenses: plane fare—or maybe a private plane!—hotel, food, and other costs for yourself and anyone else you bring along.

3. **Buy advertisements.** Television ads, social media ads, and newspaper and magazine ads all add up to a bundle. They're commonly used by candidates, political parties, and outside supporters to spread the word about election candidates. This is where the bucks really start to add up.

4. **Hire staff to coordinate all of the above activities.** Candidates for local elections might hire a few helpers and pay some expenses for volunteers. But a candidate for president might have nearly one thousand staff members working full-time, all of whom are paid by the candidate's funds. Leading up to the

Massachusetts attorney general Martha Coakley ran for governor in 2014. Her campaign raised more than $3 million.

2012 presidential election, for instance, Mitt Romney's campaign manager earned $6,500 for every two weeks of work.

As you can see, it doesn't take long before a candidate is racking up big bills to run for office.

## WHERE DOES ALL THAT MONEY COME FROM?

With national campaigns costing billions of dollars, it's impossible for even the richest of people to pay for their own campaigns. So where do candidates get the money for their campaign expenses? Candidates simply ask people for donations, and many people happily give them money. This is called fund-raising, and candidates spend a lot of their time on it. Fund-raising involves convincing other people to give money to a campaign. Candidates and their teams ask for money in five main ways:

1. **Direct mail.** A candidate's team mails letters and cards asking for donations to people who might support the campaign.
2. **Phone calls.** An adult in your household probably has received a call requesting support for one candidate or another. Political parties, candidates, or outside supporters often set up entire call centers, or warehouses with hundreds of telephone operators, to make phone calls to voters.
3. **Internet.** This includes e-mails and online ads asking for donations, as well as any websites that a campaign sets up to receive donations.
4. **Personal ask.** This is when a candidate asks people directly for money—usually wealthy people who may already be big supporters.

5. **Special events.** These include any events planned especially to encourage people to donate or ones that charge a fee to attend. These might be dinners with a candidate, concerts by big-name musicians, or gala parties thrown by supporters of the candidates.

All of these fund-raising methods can raise a lot of money. And they better, because they can also cost a lot of money. The cost of writing and mailing letters, building websites, traveling, and throwing gala events can add up quickly. The art of fund-raising is to make sure to earn more than is spent on any one method.

Rock legend Bruce Springsteen performs at a fund-raising concert for the special interest group America Coming Together. In 2004, the group raised $10 million to encourage people to vote.

## WHY DOES THE PRICE OF ELECTIONS MATTER?

If candidates are able to raise the money they need to run a campaign, why does it matter how expensive campaigns are? It's true that candidates seem to have few problems raising thousands or millions of dollars—or even a billion dollars. But there are a few reasons why people care about the costs.

One reason is that expensive elections can force candidates to spend so much time worrying about raising money that they don't have enough time to worry about what they're going to accomplish once they are elected.

Another reason is that expensive elections can be unfair for candidates who aren't personally wealthy. Even though candidates don't pay for all campaign costs themselves, having a personal fortune can still be a big advantage. It's an advantage not only because wealthy candidates can pay for more of their own costs but also because they may have more contacts and supporters who also have a lot of money. That advantage can mean that wealthier candidates are more likely to be elected.

In the United States, the government tends to be made up of wealthy citizens. One report, from the Center for Responsive Politics, found that in 2011, the median wealth of members of the US Congress was $966,001. That's a lot more than the typical American family, whose median wealth was just $68,828 in 2011.

Does that difference matter? Does anyone really care that the country's representatives are much wealthier than the average citizen? Some people don't mind at all. But when so many members of Congress are independently wealthy, other people worry that Congress will overlook the interests of lower-income citizens. These people are concerned that a very wealthy representative or senator may not understand what poorer families need from their government.

One of the biggest reasons that people are concerned about campaign funding, though, is that when some people or groups of people give money to candidates, those givers expect to get favors in return. An example of these favors might include the contributor being appointed to a special position if that candidate gets elected. For instance, President Barack Obama faced much criticism in 2009 when he appointed Louis Susman, who had helped Democrats raise hundreds of millions of dollars for recent campaigns, to be the US ambassador to the United Kingdom.

Another type of favor is expecting that a candidate, if elected, will vote for or sign laws that unfairly help a person or a group who donated. For instance, the corporation General Electric gave millions of dollars to help elect many congressional members. Once elected, most of those politicians voted in 2007 to outlaw incandescent lightbulbs. They argued that these bulbs were less energy efficient than newer bulbs on the market. Conveniently, this also allowed General Electric to sell their newer, more expensive compact fluorescent bulbs.

Whatever the favors may be, most people agree that this behavior is not very democratic, because it gives more power to people who donate money. The goal of a fair and democratic election is that every citizen's vote has the same value.

# CHAPTER TWO

# SPECIAL INTEREST GROUPS *and* LOBBYISTS

E very citizen has a stake in the outcome of elections. This includes local elections for mayors, council members, county board members, and more. It includes state elections for legislatures, judges, and governors. And it includes federal elections for members of Congress and the president. Once these public officials get elected, each of them is able to make decisions that affect the lives of voters.

Think about how the decisions made by elected officeholders might make a difference to many different people. Remember that there's always more than one side to any issue. Even if one person or a group of people are happy with a law or a policy, another person or group might be unhappy. Take a look at the following examples of possible outcomes of actions by elected officials:

Some people would be delighted if their city council approved a new stadium. Others might be disappointed.

## A city council votes to raise taxes to pay for a professional sports stadium.

### Who might be happy?

- The sports team owners who want to make more money and the players who want a nice stadium to play in
- Nearby business owners who might make new customers of stadium visitors

### Who might be unhappy?

- Taxpayers who do not want to have to pay higher taxes
- Taxpayers and government leaders who want to spend tax money for other purposes

## A mayor signs a city ordinance outlawing smoking in all public spaces.

### Who might be happy?

- Custodial workers, whose job it is to clean up dropped cigarette butts

- Parents, medical experts, and others worried about the effects of secondhand smoke

**Who might be unhappy?**

- Smokers, who might think the city is taking away their rights by telling them where they can't smoke
- Cigarette makers, who may sell fewer cigarettes to people who find it harder to smoke

## A Congress member votes to make it illegal to dump chemicals into rivers.

**Who might be happy?**

- Environmentalists who are concerned about water quality
- People who live nearby and might be getting sick from toxic water

**Who might be unhappy?**

- Owners of a manufacturing company who have to pay a lot of money to dispose of its factory chemicals rather than let them run into a nearby river

## A governor signs a state law allowing same-sex marriages.

**Who might be happy?**

- Same-sex couples who wish to marry
- People who work in the wedding industry, because they will receive more business
- People who believe everyone should have the right to marry

**Who might be unhappy?**

- People whose religious or other beliefs hold that same-sex couples should not be allowed to marry

## SPECIAL INTEREST GROUPS

As you can see, lots of people are affected by the laws and policies made by elected officials and voters. While most citizens are generally interested in the laws that affect them, many citizens have particular interests in certain areas. And when people share a common special interest, they might join together and form a group: a special interest group.

Special interest groups are also known as pressure groups, advocacy groups, or lobby groups. They are groups that come together to push for change on a certain shared interest. That interest could be religion. It could be a certain type of job. It could be the environment. Or it could be based on age, race, gender, or any number of thousands of other interests and

A special interest group is made up of people who share an interest. This group wants to draw attention to the way circus animals are treated.

## The Earliest Special Interest Group?

People with common interests have formed groups throughout history. But one of the world's first political special interest groups was formed in England in the late eighteenth century. This group of abolitionists' first official action was a 1791 boycott of sugar, which was produced by slaves. The group printed thousands of pamphlets telling people not to buy sugar and asking members of Parliament to vote to make slavery illegal. In 1805, the group circulated antislavery petitions for people to sign, and the group sent signed petitions to members of Parliament. The next year, Parliament voted to outlaw slavery.

characteristics that people have. Interest groups also come in all shapes and sizes. Some are large, and some are small. Some—the most successful—are extremely active, buying television ads and other high-profile communications. Some are so quiet that many people outside the group don't know about them.

One thing all special interest groups have in common is their desire to affect laws or policies in their interest area. Sometimes they want to change current laws, and sometimes they want to keep existing laws in place.

Interest groups get their power from their members. The more people who support a special interest—and tell politicians that they support it—the more likely a politician is to vote the way the interest group wants. Politicians know that people will vote against them or their party in the next election if they don't go along with the group's wishes. Since there are almost always many sides to each issue, politicians often get pressure from several different groups about the same issue.

Sometimes special interest groups work to pass or defeat a ballot initiative that is part of an election. That means voters are asked to vote yes or no on a specific question, such as "Should same-sex marriage be legal in this city (or state)?" In that case, the groups are trying to convince people how to vote on the ballot question rather than who to vote for.

## WHAT KINDS OF ISSUES DO SPECIAL INTEREST GROUPS WORK ON?

| ISSUE | INTEREST-GROUP EXAMPLES |
| --- | --- |
| Animal rights | People for the Ethical Treatment of Animals (PETA) |
| Helium supply | The Balloon Council |
| Civil rights and equality for all people | The National Association for the Advancement of Colored People (NAACP), the Mexican-American Legal Defense and Education Fund (MALDEF), and the Human Rights Campaign |
| Decrease regulations on businesses | US Chamber of Commerce |
| Gun limits and rights to gun ownership | Coalition to Stop Gun Violence, National Rifle Association |
| Medicare and health care | AARP, 60 Plus Association, American Public Health Association, American Medical Association, America's Health Insurance Plans, Citizens' Council for Health Freedom, Physicians for a National Health Program |
| Protecting the environment | Sierra Club |
| Treatment of captured reptiles | The US Association of Reptile Keepers |
| Worker protections, such as the right to be notified of a layoff | American Federation of Labor and Congress of Industrial Organization (AFL-CIO) |

# SPECIAL INTEREST GROUPS

## PROS:

- Special interest groups can help inform voters about issues voters might not be aware of.

- Special interests can represent people whose voices might not otherwise be heard in an election.

- Special interests help people exercise their freedom of speech, or their right to let politicians know their thoughts on issues.

## CONS:

- Special interest groups can "buy" legislation. Once elected, officials may vote to help those groups because they owe the group, not because the legislation is best for most citizens.

- Special interest groups with the most money can have an unfair advantage. Groups that represent minorities often have less money and therefore less influence.

- Special interests can limit freedom of speech, in that they might keep those who don't have enough money or power to form an interest group from being heard.

## HOW DO SPECIAL INTEREST GROUPS INFLUENCE ELECTIONS?

Elected officials aren't the only people whom special interest groups try to influence. These groups also have a big interest in people who aren't yet elected. That is, they want to make sure that whoever supports their position gets elected. And for that reason, special interest groups pay a lot of attention to elections.

How do these groups influence elections? Here are some examples:

- **Contribute money to candidates' campaigns.** The simplest way that a special interest group helps a candidate get elected is to give money. The campaign uses the money to pay for advertising, travel, and other expenses.
- **Endorse a single candidate.** Often a special interest group will give formal approval to a specific candidate and encourage its members and supporters to vote for that candidate. The group may communicate this through letters or e-mails to its members, television or other ads, or other media announcements.

### Playing Both Sides

It probably makes sense that special interest groups would give money to a candidate that supports their group. But many groups give money to more than one candidate running in an election. That way, whoever wins will feel some debt toward the group—and be more willing to support laws in the group's favor.

The NAACP is a civil rights–focused special interest group. This protester was part of a group asking South Carolina to remove a Confederate flag on government property.

- **Continue to contact candidates once they are elected.** This is usually called lobbying. Special interest groups often have their own lobbyists, who encourage elected officials to support the group's issues. Lobbyists meet with politicians to share information about their special interests, and they also remind the politicians that they supported their election. Maybe more importantly, the groups remind officials that they may or may not support the official in the next election.

# CHAPTER THREE

# CONTRIBUTION LIMITS and SOFT MONEY

S pecial interest groups and the lobbyists who work for them are big players in elections. Most people agree that it's important to have laws governing exactly how these players—and their money—can influence elections. These laws are called campaign finance regulations, or campaign finance reform laws. Although this topic is frequently in the news, it isn't new. The role of money in elections has been a concern since the earliest days of the United States. By the turn of the twentieth century, the idea of campaign finance reform was getting serious attention.

Three basic components make up campaign finance reform laws. A single law can include just one of these, or it can be made up of two or three parts. The first is campaign contribution limits. These limit the amount of money that individuals or groups can donate to candidates. Campaign spending rules, the next type of laws, focus on how donated money can be spent during an election and what candidates can spend it on. A third type of reform law is called disclosure rules. These laws require candidates to tell

Many special interest groups cannot give money directly to candidates or elected officials. But lobbyists who work for these groups meet personally with officials to ask for support of the groups' goals.

the public exactly how much money they received and from whom they received it.

## EARLY CONTRIBUTION RESTRICTIONS

Placing limits on the amount of money that individuals or groups can donate to campaigns is a basic tool of campaign finance reform. One of the biggest concerns has always been that successful companies could "buy" government policies by donating money to political campaigns. In return, company owners might expect that politicians would pass laws favoring businesses.

The first real contribution limits for US elections were passed in 1907, when the Tillman Act prohibited certain businesses from donating to federal political campaigns. The Tillman Act seemed great, but in reality, there wasn't an easy way to enforce it. So businesses continued to donate to many campaigns, which in turn meant that people continued to be upset.

Many people also thought the Tillman Act was unfair because it only barred businesses from giving money to campaigns. Meanwhile, the unions that represented workers were allowed to give as much as they wanted. People thought this put business owners at a disadvantage. If politicians received money from workers' groups but not from business owners, politicians might pass more laws that favored workers. These might be laws that gave workers higher wages or more benefits, or other rules that could cost business owners money.

In 1943, the Smith-Connally Act aimed to level the playing field by banning unions from donating to federal campaigns as

## President Roosevelt and the Earliest Campaign Finance Reform

Shortly after his election in 1904, President Theodore Roosevelt *(below)* called for banning corporate contributions in a famous speech before Congress:

"All contributions by corporations to any political committee or for any political purpose should be forbidden by law; directors should not be permitted to use stockholders' money for such purposes; and, moreover, a prohibition of this kind would be, as far as it went, an effective method of stopping the evils aimed at in corrupt practices acts."

well. That meant companies and unions had basically the same limits. Still, the laws were hard to enforce and large campaign donations continued.

## THE BIRTH OF PACs

These early campaign finance laws left businesses, labor unions, and other special interest groups with a problem. These groups, unions, and businesses really wanted to have some say in who was elected to office, but the law said they couldn't donate any money. What could they do? One solution came in the form of political action committees (PACs).

PACs have been around since the 1940s. PACs are organizations set up by a group for the specific purpose of helping candidates get elected. Since PACs are not the same as the business, the labor union, or the other group that set them up, they are allowed to donate to campaigns. But they are often started by individuals who also own companies or lead unions.

In case you are thinking that PACs sound sneaky, they are perfectly legal. But by the early 1970s, people were concerned that PACs allowed wealthy people and interest groups to have too much influence on election outcomes. They provided a way around the laws that governed how much businesses could donate to campaigns.

## GETTING SERIOUS ABOUT CAMPAIGN FINANCE REFORM

The Federal Election Campaign Act of 1971 and amendments to it in 1974 aimed to close the PAC loophole by setting limits on how much money PACs could raise and how much they could contribute. The Federal Election Campaign Act spells out exactly how much money a PAC can raise and how much it can donate.

In federal elections, any individual is allowed to donate up to $5,000 per year to a PAC. And in turn, each PAC can give up to $5,000 per year to a candidate and $15,000 to a political party.

The Federal Election Campaign Act also required PACs to disclose, or tell the public, the names of the people who gave them money as well as how they spent that money. That allows voters to learn who is actually funding certain campaigns. Anyone can look up information on the US government's Disclosure Data Search on the Federal Election Commission's website.

The Federal Election Campaign Act had one more important piece. It created a new agency to enforce campaign finance laws: the Federal Election Commission (FEC). The FEC's job was and still is to make sure that candidates and the people who donate to their campaigns follow the laws about contribution limits, spending limits, and disclosure. The FEC puts out reports by every candidate for Congress or for the presidency. These reports list how much each campaign has raised and spent. They also include the name, the address, the employer, and the job title of everyone who donated more than $200 to one of those campaigns.

## SOFT MONEY AND OTHER LOOPHOLES

The Federal Election Campaign Act laws about contribution limits apply to any money that's donated directly to candidates or political parties for spending on elections. This strictly controlled money is known as "hard money."

But the laws left a little wiggle room, often called a loophole. Money that political parties use for nonelection activities, such as registering voters or encouraging them to come out and vote on Election Day, was not so tightly regulated. Contributions to these activities are called soft money. In the 1970s laws, there were no limits on how much soft money the

## Why Disclosure Rules Matter

Disclosure rules, or the requirements that candidates and special interest groups publicly report who gave them money, are sometimes called the heart of campaign finance reform. Why does making that information public matter so much?

First, when voters have information about where money came from and how it was spent, they can make better choices. For instance, if an environmental group donated a lot of money to a campaign, a voter might expect the candidate to vote in favor of environmental issues. If a voter feels strongly one way or the other on a current environmental issue, that information could affect her vote.

Second, when the public knows who a politician received money from, they can be more aware of whether that politician is doing special favors for the supporter. For example, suppose a big oil company gives a lot of money to an Alaskan senator's campaign. Then that senator, once elected, introduces a bill to increase oil drilling in Alaska. Who does that bill help? Who does it hurt? Does that bill represent the needs of that senator's constituents? Does it affect any other people in Alaska?

Finally, having accurate reports of who donated what to whom helps to enforce all other campaign finance laws. Knowing those arguments, what do you think? Does disclosure help voters? Can you think of any other reasons for or against disclosure rules?

people, labor unions, businesses, or other groups could give to political parties. Political parties did and still do collect lots of soft money each year.

Political parties weren't and still aren't allowed to spend soft money to support candidates in an election—but they are allowed to spend it on nonelection activities. But the Federal Election Campaign Act also left a lot of wiggle room with soft money. For instance, a political party couldn't use soft money to pay for a television ad that directly asked people to vote for a certain candidate. But it could pay for an ad that showed a picture of a candidate and told voters to "Get out and vote on Election Day!" To a lot of people, those two kinds of ads were too close for comfort.

A 2002 law known as the McCain-Feingold Act addressed this soft-money loophole. The law placed very strict limits on how political parties could raise and spend soft money. Specifically, it limited the amount of money that interest groups and political parties are allowed to contribute directly to campaigns. When the law was passed, the hope was that it would greatly change the role of money in elections. However, just as with past attempts to reform campaign finance, interest groups soon found new loopholes to help them spend large sums of money to help elect candidates.

Campaign Finance

Senators John McCain *(left)* and Russ Feingold *(right)* sponsored the Bipartisan Campaign Reform Act of 2002, often called the McCain-Feingold Act. The goal of this law was to limit how much money special interest groups could give to election campaigns.

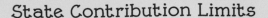

## State Contribution Limits

The Federal Election Campaign Act, the McCain-Feingold Act, and the other laws discussed here apply to federal elections. But most states also have laws about campaign donations for state and local elections.

Thirty-eight states have limits on how much money individuals can donate to a candidate. These limits vary from state to state, but in 2011, the average limit for donating to a campaign for governor—the highest state office—was approximately $8,500. For state house or senate elections in 2013, the average limit was approximately $3,500.

All but six states also have limits on how much money businesses can donate to campaigns. Twenty-one states ban those donations altogether, and twenty-five states place limits on donation amounts.

## 527s AND 501(c)(4)s

Some organizations have numbers for names, such as 527s and 501(c)(4)s. These are two types of nonprofit groups behind most of the soft money spent on elections. They spend a lot of money, but they don't give it directly to candidates, campaigns, or political parties. Instead, these groups pay for activities, such as encouraging people to vote or making ads about issues instead of individual candidates.

Similar to most types of nonprofit groups in the United States, 527s and 501(c)(4)s are named after numbers in the national tax laws. The numbers refer to the line in the tax law that describes the rules for each type of nonprofit. For instance, 527s can be formed specifically to influence election outcomes. They're usually formed by wealthy people, businesses, unions, or other special interest groups. These nonprofit groups are allowed to donate money to campaigns, and in return, 527s must report their activities to the government. This means the public can see who has donated to these groups and how much they have donated.

As with most special interest groups, 527s can be liberal, conservative, or have elements of both. A 527 can be a PAC if it agrees to follow PAC rules, but it does not have to be a PAC. One well-known example of a 527 is EMILY'S List. This group's main goal is to elect pro-choice female Democratic candidates. In 2014, the 527 spent nearly $10 million. About $330,000 of this was on media, including advertising and media consultants.

Another type of nonprofit group is 501(c)(4)s, which work to promote social welfare. This might be charity, education, or recreation activities aimed at improving people's lives. Frequently, these groups also work to influence elections or get certain candidates elected. Legally, though, that can't be their main focus. And since 501(c)(4)s are not focused on election activities, they are not restricted by campaign finance laws, such as the ones requiring that all campaign donors' names are reported to the public.

## RULES FOR NONPROFIT CAMPAIGN FUNDING ORGANIZATIONS

|  | 527 | 501(C)(4) |
|---|---|---|
| Allowed to spend money to influence elections? | Yes, this is their primary focus. | Yes, but it can't be their primary purpose. |
| Allowed to raise unlimited sums of money? | Yes | Yes |
| Limits on how much money individual people can donate? | No | No |
| Have to publicly report who gives them money? | Yes | No |

Again, these groups can be conservative, liberal, or somewhere in between. Unlike 527 groups, a 501(c)(4) cannot be a PAC. The National Rifle Association (NRA) Foundation is one example of a 501(c)(4). This group's main goal is to teach people to safely use firearms. But its leaders also spend money to try to influence gun ownership laws.

## OPPOSING VIEWPOINTS: ON A 2014 PROPOSED AMENDMENT TO REGULATE CAMPAIGN FUNDING

**PRO**

"There should not be a million-dollar entry fee for participating in our democracy. I oppose the notion that a big bank account should give billionaires, corporations or special interest groups a greater place in government than American voters."
—Harry Reid, Democratic senator from Nevada, May 15, 2014

"For over two centuries, Congress has not dared to mess with the Bill of Rights. This amendment, if adopted, would give Congress absolute authority to regulate the political speech of every single American, with no limitations whatsoever."
—Ted Cruz, Republican senator from Texas, June 3, 2014

**CON**

# CHAPTER FOUR

# FREE SPEECH, ADVERTISING, and SUPER PACS

When it comes to how special interest groups influence elections, there are plenty of laws and loopholes. But in addition to the many rules about donations—and the equally many loopholes for getting around those rules—there's one very important issue. It's freedom of speech. Freedom of speech is the basic human right to voice one's opinions, without fear of getting in trouble for what you say. In the United States, free speech is protected by the First Amendment to the Constitution.

## WHAT DOES FREE SPEECH HAVE TO DO WITH ELECTIONS?

In the United States, voting is often thought to be the ultimate expression of free speech. Have you ever heard anyone suggest that if you don't vote, you can't be upset by anything government officials do? Many people believe that voting means expressing your opinion about who you want to represent you in your government. You have a right to vote

In the United States, citizens vote as part of their right to speak and express their beliefs freely.

for whomever you want, and you can't get in trouble for how you vote.

The right to free speech also includes the right to tell others why you support or don't support a candidate in an election. In some places in the world, people are jailed, tortured, or even killed for expressing opinions about how government should be run. But in the United States and many other democracies, people are allowed to express those opinions. Their right to free speech is designed to protect them.

Free speech also protects people's rights to spend money trying to convince others how to vote. But, as you've learned, campaign finance laws limit the amount of money people can spend to support candidates in elections. Some people think these laws are fair because they keep wealthy people from having more of a say in government, or a bigger right to free speech, than those with less money. Others think the laws are unfair because they limit big spenders' expression of free speech.

A loophole still exists for people who want to spend more money than what is legally allowed. The loophole is this: while there's a limit to how much money a person can donate to a candidate or a group, there's no limit on how much money the same person can spend. So that person can donate to many different candidates, rather than just one. The loophole also means people can make their own expensive advertisements to help candidates. Those people must pay for the ads themselves, instead of giving the money to a candidate to make the ad.

## WHAT DOES FREE SPEECH HAVE TO DO WITH SPECIAL INTEREST GROUPS?

Free speech has plenty to do with special interest groups. Every time an interest group tries to convince voters to vote for a certain candidate, that interest group is exercising its right to free speech. The campaign finance laws of the early 1970s limited how much money interest groups can donate to political campaigns. But, protected by free-speech laws, groups have long been allowed to make their own ads supporting candidates.

By the early 2000s, some people were worried, again, that those free-speech laws gave too much influence to wealthy people and groups. So the 2002 McCain-Feingold Act set some new rules to try to limit the influence. In addition to the soft money limits, this act created rules about advertisements. One rule was that special interest groups, businesses, and unions couldn't run ads promoting a candidate within sixty days of a general election or within thirty days of a primary election.

## "And I Approve This Message"

Have you ever heard "and I approve this message" at the end of an election ad? Maybe you've noticed those words at the end of *many* political ads. That's not by chance. It's a law. It's called the "Stand by Your Ad" rule and it was part of the 2002 McCain-Feingold Act. It requires all television or radio ads made by a candidate for federal office to include "a statement by the candidate that identifies the candidate and states that the candidate has approved the communication." The point is to make candidates take responsibility for the statements they advertise. So since the 2004 elections, you frequently hear, "I'm Candidate X, and I approve this message." If a group not affiliated with a candidate makes an ad, that group must end the ad by clearly stating or displaying the name of the person or the group that made the advertisement.

## MEDIA, FREE SPEECH, AND THE CITIZENS UNITED COURT CASE

Newspapers, books, movies, and other media often spread information and opinions about political candidates and other election issues. Some media try to directly convince voters whom to vote for. Special interest groups often create and pay for media with the specific intent of convincing voters to vote for or against a candidate or a ballot measure. Those kinds of communications are perfectly legal. They are protected by free speech. But in some cases, it can be hard to tell if a video clip is an entertainment piece—such as a short movie—or an ad.

With the McCain-Feingold Act in mind, a nonprofit group called Citizens United that supports Republican issues filed a complaint with the FEC in 2004 against the movie *Fahrenheit 9/11.* This film, by director Michael Moore, criticized the way President George W. Bush had handled the events of September 11, 2001. On that day, a group called al-Qaeda led attacks on the United States that killed nearly three thousand people. Eighteen months later, the United States invaded Iraq. Citizens United said it should be illegal to run ads for the movie within sixty days of an election. But the FEC didn't agree with Citizens United. The FEC said the ads did not break the law.

Citizens United decided to make its own movie. The nonprofit made *Hillary: The Movie*, which tried to convince voters not to vote for Hillary Clinton in the 2008 Democratic primary. But this time, the FEC decided that this was breaking the law. It banned the group from showing ads for the movie close to the primaries. Citizens United took the decision to court. The case, called *Citizens United v. Federal Election Commission*, was actually heard by several courts. During this time, many different aspects of campaign finance regulation, not just how close to an election ads can be shown, were added to the discussion.

In 2010, the US Supreme Court—the highest court in the country and the final say on all court cases—ruled on *Citizens United v. Federal Election Commission*. The court ruled that the law banning political ads from being shown within sixty days of an election was a violation of people's right to free

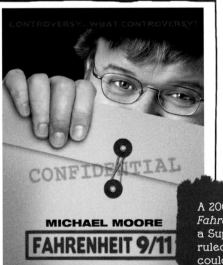

A 2004 lawsuit over the movie *Fahrenheit 9/11* eventually led to a Supreme Court case. The court ruled in 2010 that political ads could run at any time, even just before an election.

speech. The decision was a surprise to many people—and a blow to supporters of campaign finance reform.

## FROM PACS TO SUPER PACS

The *Citizens United v. Federal Election Commission* decision didn't change the biggest issue in campaign finance: contribution limits. But it paved the way for big changes.

**OPPOSING VIEWPOINTS: ON THE 2010 *CITIZENS UNITED V. FEDERAL ELECTION COMISSION* RULING**

"Limits on political contributions have never fulfilled their intended purposes, and never will. I believe that contributions are, indeed, speech, and that transparency and full disclosure allow voters and the public to make their own decisions as to the propriety of a candidate's sources of funding."
—Gary Johnson, New Mexico governor, October 9, 2012

"I don't think American elections should be bankrolled by America's most powerful interests, or worse, by foreign entities. They should be decided by the American people."
—Barack Obama, president, January 10, 2010

Less than three months later, the DC Circuit Court of Appeals ruled on another campaign finance case: *SpeechNow.org vs. Federal Election Commission*. In that decision, the court said that people and groups could make unlimited donations to PACs as long as the PAC didn't work directly with a candidate's campaign.

That requirement—that to accept unlimited donations, a PAC can't coordinate directly with a candidate or a political party—led to a new type of PAC. Officially, these groups are called independent expenditure-only committees, but they are known as super PACs. Super PACs are allowed to accept unlimited donations from people and groups—and to spend unlimited amounts to try to influence elections. They just can't coordinate with candidates or campaigns when they do things such as make ads and send e-mails. The idea is that super PACs allow people to exercise their right to free speech—and, by extension, people's right to spend their money to express their opinions.

Super PACs also have to report the names of everyone who gives them money. By disclosing where the money comes from, groups are keeping the public informed. The idea is that this keeps people, groups, and businesses honest: they can't say they support one thing (such as protecting the environment) but then secretly give money to a candidate who supports an opposing idea (such as allowing factories to dump chemicals in rivers).

Super PACs are intended to balance people's right to free speech with the public's right to know who is funding candidates' campaigns. But many people think the rules about super PACs are too loose. It can be hard to define exactly what it means to "coordinate directly" with a candidate. For instance, in the 2012 presidential election, a former aide to Obama headed a super PAC working to reelect him. And the

## Did the *Citizens United v. Federal Election Commission* Decision "Create" Super PACs?

It's commonly said that the US Supreme Court's ruling in the *Citizens United* case created super PACs. But that's not entirely true. What is true is that the court drew a line between PACs—which have been around for decades—that do or do not coordinate directly with a candidate. If a PAC coordinates with a candidate, the court said, it can only accept contributions of up to $5,000 from individual people. But if a PAC does not coordinate with a candidate, then they can accept unlimited contributions from individuals—as well as from corporations, unions, and other groups. Super PACs grew out of this distinction. They are, basically, ordinary PACs that make sure to not coordinate directly with a candidate. Does that mean they can't affect elections? Not really—these groups can and do spend millions of dollars on ads for and against candidates. They just produce them on their own, without technically coordinating with a candidate.

super PAC working to elect Romney was headed by a former Romney aide.

## ANONYMOUS GIVING: THE RISE OF "DARK" MONEY

People have strong opinions about the *Citizens United* ruling and about super PACs. But like them or not, there's no doubt that they make the rules pretty clear: if someone wants to donate money to help a candidate in a federal election, four options are available. You can give money to any of the following:

- **A candidate.** You can give up to $2,600 per candidate per election, and your name as a donor is available to the public.
- **A PAC.** You can give up to $5,000 to any one group per election, and your name is made public.

- **A political party.** As of 2014, according to a congressional bill passed that year, you can give up to $324,000 per calendar year and your name is made public.
- **A super PAC.** You can give as much money as you want, and your name is made public.

You might notice the reason why super PACs are such a big deal. Of all the options, they are the only one that has no limits on the size of contributions. That makes these groups the obvious choice for wealthy people and groups who want to donate a lot of money during an election.

Do you notice anything that all four of the above options have in common? They all require that the names of the people who donated money are publicly available.

However, lots of people and groups do not want the public to know whom they gave money to. They want to remain anonymous. This might be because they are supporting an unpopular cause. Or it could be because they are giving money to opposing candidates.

So what do donors do when they want to donate a lot of money and remain anonymous? Remember those nonprofit groups known as 501(c)(4)s? They are also called social welfare nonprofits, because helping people has to be their main focus. However, these groups are also allowed to spend money to influence elections. They might mail brochures, produce ads, make phone calls, or spread the word about issues in other ways. These nonprofits are allowed to accept unlimited donations to fund those activities. And most importantly—at least to people who want to give anonymously—501(c)(4)s don't have to report the names of their donors, unlike super PACs.

It worries many people that these nonprofit groups are able to accept and spend so much money on elections. They

## Seriously Mocking the Super PAC

In 2011, comedian Stephen Colbert of the television channel Comedy Central took on the issue of how difficult it is to keep a super PAC from coordinating with a candidate. Colbert started a fictional super PAC called Americans for a Better Tomorrow, Tomorrow. Then he announced he was going to run for president of South Carolina. Under super PAC rules, the super PAC couldn't coordinate directly with Colbert the candidate, so Colbert passed off control of the super PAC to another Comedy Central comedian, Jon Stewart. Stewart renamed the super PAC the Definitely Not Coordinating with Stephen Colbert Super PAC. He famously claimed, "Stephen and I have in no way worked out a series of Morse-code blinks to convey information with each other on our respective shows."

worry that these groups have the ability to sway voters to vote certain ways, without the voters knowing who is really supporting the group. This type of election spending is known as dark money. And since 2010, it has grown incredibly quickly. In the 2012 election, for instance, the group Americans for Prosperity spent nearly $34 million opposing Obama's reelection. During the same election, the League of Conservation Voters spent millions of dollars supporting Democratic candidates. One estimate shows that total spending by 501(c)(4)s grew from approximately $86 million during the 2008 presidential elections to $257 million in the next presidential elections of 2012.

## SUPER PACS

## PROS:

- Super PACs protect free speech by allowing people and groups to donate as much money as they want to influence an election.

- Super PACs protect the public's right to know who is giving money by requiring reports of donors' names.

## CONS:

- Super PACs make it possible for money to buy influence over citizens' opinions.

- It can be very hard to make sure a super PAC and a campaign aren't coordinating directly, which means this rule probably gets broken.

# CHAPTER FIVE

# PUBLIC FUNDING INITIATIVES

T he United States has a long history of campaign finance reform. Many laws and court rulings on the issue have a similar goal: to keep elections fair. They aim to protect people's right to vote while limiting the power of any one group on an election's outcome. These laws spell out how much money people are able to donate, how that money can be spent, and how public the records of the donors should be.

Another area of campaign finance reform is the idea of publicly funded elections. In short, this means that the government gives candidates a set amount of money to use in campaigns. In return, the candidates who accept the government money agree to a limit on how much extra money they are allowed to raise.

## THE HISTORY OF PUBLIC FUNDING FOR CAMPAIGNS

The idea for providing public funding for elections goes all the way back to 1907—the year the Tillman Act first banned corporations from donating to political campaigns. That year,

President Theodore Roosevelt also recommended a complete ban on individual donations to campaigns and that the federal government provide funds for candidates instead. But the issue didn't catch the interest of voters, and politicians soon dropped it.

Almost sixty years passed before public financing became law. In 1966, Congress passed the first public funding law. Under that law, the government would give money to the major political parties during a presidential election. Candidates running for president would then get money from their political parties. A year later, though, Congress voted to suspend the law, so it never led to real changes.

In 1971, public funding laws really did get rolling. That year, Congress passed a law similar to the 1966 law. But in this version, the government money went directly to the candidate instead of to the political party. This law, called the Revenue Act, also placed limits on how much money presidential

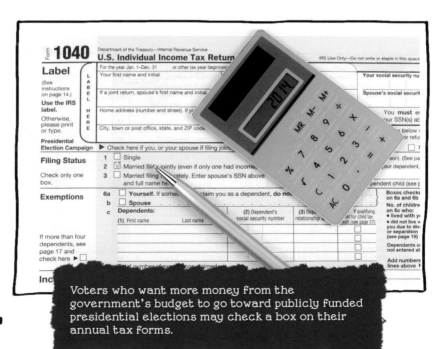

Voters who want more money from the government's budget to go toward publicly funded presidential elections may check a box on their annual tax forms.

candidates who receive public money could spend, and it banned the candidates from receiving any private donations. A few years later, in 1974, the law was changed to include public funding for presidential primary elections and for the nominating conventions held by the major parties.

Under the law, the FEC oversees the public funding program. It did this for the first time in 1976. Eligible presidential candidates used federal funds in their primary and general election campaigns, and the major parties used public funds to pay for their nominating conventions. A few smaller changes have been made over the years, but the modern election funding program remains basically the same.

## WHERE DOES PUBLIC FUNDING MONEY COME FROM?

Similar to all government money, public election funds come from taxes. When voters fill out their federal tax returns, they have the option to check a box for a Presidential Election Campaign Fund. If they check that box, three dollars go to the fund. (Until 1993, that amount was one dollar.) If they don't check the box, no money goes to the fund. Either way, the person pays the same amount in taxes—the three dollars isn't added to the person's tax bill. Checking the box just means that three dollars more from the government's overall budget will go to the Presidential Election Campaign Fund.

So taxpayers pay the whole cost of elections in a publicly funded election system. Some think that's a good idea, and some think it's a bad idea. Supporters of public funding say that elections are an important part of democracy, so the government should pay for them. These people consider it a reasonable cost of government and believe the money is spent on informing the public about their choices in the election. That, they say, is a public good.

But other people oppose public funding of elections. They say that if someone wants to run for election, that candidate should be able and willing to do the work to raise the money needed to win over voters. And opponents say that it's not fair to make people pay extra taxes for campaigns. After all, even if someone doesn't check the box on a tax return, some of that person's tax dollars still pay for campaigning.

## HOW DOES PUBLIC FUNDING WORK?

There are two main types of public funding for elections. One kind is often called a partial public fund program. In a partial public fund program, usually used by states, the government gives money to qualified candidates to pay for some but not all of their campaign expenses. Many states offer a partial matching fund program for state elections. This means a candidate gets a certain amount of public money for each dollar raised from private contributions.

Sometimes, partial funding is based on a block grant system. This means the government provides a lump-sum payment to each candidate who meets specific requirements. The requirements usually include raising a minimum amount of private contributions. This is a way for candidates to prove that they have a certain amount of support among voters.

The other type of public funding is full public financing. The public funding system for the presidential general election is an example. A few states also allow candidates in state races to qualify for full public funding. States often use the term *Clean Elections* to describe this idea. Under this system, the government provides money to candidates to pay for nearly all of their campaign expenses. In exchange, the candidates agree not to accept any private campaign contributions other than a small amount needed to get their campaign started.

# Partial Matching Funds in the Presidential Primary

The law that allows public funding of the presidential primary election uses a partial matching funds system. Basically, the government offers candidates matching payments. It will match up to $250 donated by any person. Each person's total contributions count only once. For instance, if a person makes several $250 contributions, the government won't match all of them.

Candidates also have to show that they have a certain amount of support before they can receive matching funds. Each candidate must raise more than $5,000 in each of at least twenty states. In total, a candidate has to raise more than $100,000. And that money has to come from many different supporters. So even though an individual voter may give up to $2,600 to a primary candidate, no more than $250 from any one voter can count toward the $5,000 the candidate needs to earn in a state.

To collect the matching funds, candidates must be seeking a nomination to run for president by an established political party. In addition, as of 2014, the candidates have to agree to three conditions. First, a candidate must limit campaign spending for all primary elections to $10 million. This is called the national spending limit. Second, a candidate must limit campaign spending in each state to $200,000. There are exceptions for some of the states with the largest populations—candidates are allowed to spend more in those states. Finally, the candidate must limit spending of her or his own personal money to $50,000.

The campaign finance law leaves some expenses out of the spending limits. Certain fund-raising expenses and legal and accounting expenses used only to ensure the campaign obeys the law do not count against the limits.

To qualify for full public financing, candidates also have to meet certain requirements. There's one set of rules for the presidential general election (see "Public Funding in the Presidential General Election," *below*). States that use this system have different rules. In general, candidates have to raise a certain number of small contributions to show they have support. This shows that a large number of voters support the candidate. At the same time, it keeps the total money raised very low.

## Public Funding in the Presidential General Election

The presidential nominee of each of the major political parties can receive $20 million for campaigning in the general election. Accepting this money means candidates don't do as much fund-raising as they would otherwise. They can spend a little additional money, though, within certain guidelines. The first is that candidates may spend up to $50,000 from their own personal funds. That money doesn't count against the $20 million spending limit. Also, candidates can spend additional money on activities that help them comply with campaign finance laws. This might include keeping records of their expenses and other tasks. Candidates can raise private money for those expenses, as long as they keep it in a separate bank account.

These full public funding rules apply only to candidates who win the nomination of one of the two major parties, the Republicans or the Democrats. But other candidates can still qualify for partial public funding of their general election campaigns if they represent a party that's considered a minor political party, such as the Green or Independent parties. To achieve this, the party must have received between 5 and 25 percent of the total popular vote in the last presidential election. Those candidates may accept and spend private contributions along with whatever public funding they qualify for—it's based on how much of the vote their party won in the last election.

George W. Bush was the first major party candidate in twenty-four years to decline public funding for his primary election campaign in 2000.

## THE SUCCESS OF PUBLIC FUNDING?

Federal public financing got its official start in the 1976 presidential election. That year, President Gerald Ford and challenger Jimmy Carter both accepted public funding for both their primary and general election campaigns. For the next five elections—through the 1996 election—all major party candidates also voluntarily accepted public funding for both the primary and general elections.

In 2000, George W. Bush became the first major party candidate to decide not to accept public funds for the primary election. That's the election when voters decide on a candidate from each party to go on to the general election. His reasoning was simple math: he would have qualified for $16.5 million in matching public funds, but he would have been limited to $40 million in spending. And since he'd already raised more than three-quarters of that, he said it didn't make any sense to accept public matching. He did, however, accept public funding for the 2000 general election. But in 2004, Bush again rejected public money during the primaries and two Democratic

# PUBLIC FUNDING REPLACING PRIVATE CAMPAIGN FUND-RAISING

## PROS:

- Public funding allows candidates to spend more time talking with voters and less time fund-raising.

- Candidates won't have obligations to pass laws that favor their biggest donors . . . or repay favors in other ways.

- Public funding allows candidates who don't have much money or support from wealthy special interest groups to enter races.

## CONS:

- Without special interest groups spending money to influence voters, the public may be less aware of or informed about issues.

- Public funding forces all taxpayers to pay for campaigning, even if they have no interest in an election.

- Some people believe there are more important causes to spend public tax money on than elections.

candidates followed his lead: Howard Dean and John Kerry. By 2008, Democrat Hillary Clinton and Republicans John McCain, Ron Paul, Rudy Giuliani, and Mitt Romney all opted out of public funding for the primaries.

During the 2008 general presidential election, Democrat Barack Obama chose not to use public financing. In 2012, both major party candidates—Obama and Republican Mitt Romney—declined to take public funds for the general election. The skyrocketing cost of elections—due mostly to the increase of special interest–funded ads—seemed to have made it too difficult to stick to the spending limits that public funding calls for. Candidates wanted to be able to raise and spend as much as they could. By the 2016 elections, no one seriously expected any major party candidates to accept public funding. Even supporters of the idea were saying that it needed a complete overhaul if it was ever going to be successful again.

# CHAPTER SIX

# THE CHANGING LANDSCAPE of FUND-RAISING

The Internet has changed many things about elections in the United States. Until the early 1990s, voters heard from political candidates and the groups that support them in three main ways. They were visited by door knockers, who spoke about an issue and dropped off printed information about candidates. Voters also received phone calls or mail from candidates, parties, and special interest groups. And most of them saw and heard plenty of ads on television, on radio, in newspapers, or via other media. People often complained about the overabundance of information being broadcast to them.

During modern election seasons, voters often still feel bombarded by mail, phone calls, and in-person visits. People who watch network television still see plenty of ads. But there's a whole additional channel for campaign communication: the Internet. Modern citizens are constantly seeing websites, e-mails, Facebook posts, tweets, videos, and updates pertaining to candidates and political issues. People

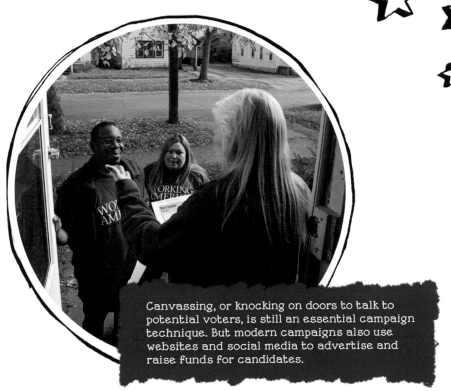

Canvassing, or knocking on doors to talk to potential voters, is still an essential campaign technique. But modern campaigns also use websites and social media to advertise and raise funds for candidates.

also get opinions from friends on the Internet. In addition, voters may be getting facts and propaganda from candidates and the political parties or special interest groups that support them. And many people are probably getting plenty of requests for money to support those candidates.

Obama's 2008 and 2012 presidential campaigns are often noted as having turned election fund-raising upside down. What does that mean? In the past, campaigns had focused on bringing in a smaller number of large-dollar donations from wealthy supporters. Instead, organizers of Obama's campaign asked for—and received—many small online donations. With the help of websites, e-mail, social media, and text messaging, Obama raised an estimated $403 million in 2008 and $504 million in 2012.

So is it true that social media and other online activity are turning campaign fund-raising—and elections—upside down?

How are special interest groups and other election players using technology? And finally, is that helping or hurting the electoral process?

## SPECIAL INTEREST GROUPS ONLINE

Special interest groups of all sizes use the Internet to influence elections. This includes groups such as PACs and 527s, whose specific purpose is to influence elections. It also includes groups such as 501(c)(4)s, which aren't allowed to spend most of their time or money on elections but which do plenty of campaign work nonetheless.

Small or large, poor or well-funded, special interest groups almost always have websites, blogs, lengthy e-mail lists of supporters, and Facebook, Twitter, and other social media profiles. They use all of these methods for sharing information—with their members or supporters and the general public. These groups spread the word about issues being debated in Congress, state legislatures, or local councils. They're also spreading the word about important issues in federal, state, and local elections.

Interest groups also go online to recruit new members or supporters and to encourage their current members or supporters to share information further. To do this, a group might write a blog post, tweet, post a Facebook status, or reach out on whatever social media platform is favored by the people the group is trying to reach. A group might send a very specific message, such as "Here's why you should vote for candidate X," or "This is why candidate Y is terrible." Or a group might share information on why citizens should vote yes or no on a ballot measure.

Once the ideas are posted publicly, groups often ask their supporters to share the information. According to one survey, this works well: in 2012, 30 percent of registered voters said

Barack Obama was the first major presidential candidate to really dive into social media. As of 2015, his Twitter feed had 54.7 million followers.

they had been encouraged to vote one way or the other by posts on social media sites such as Facebook or Twitter. And one-third of all social media users had shared, or reposted, content about a political or social issue.

Special interest groups also use the Internet to ask for contributions. For raising money, e-mail—along with traditional methods of phone calls and direct mail—is the most common approach. A typical e-mail might ask for a very small contribution, state a reason why it's urgent to contribute right away, and provide a direct link to a website that will take a donation. Using social media such as Facebook or Twitter to ask for contributions remains less common but is growing.

## THE FUTURE OF SPECIAL INTEREST GROUPS, ONLINE FUND-RAISING, AND ELECTIONS

Campaigns, political parties, and special interest groups all have great reasons to communicate online with their constituents. They can quickly reach a very wide audience using websites, e-mail, or any number of other tools. An interest group can prepare a printed ad, a video, or a press release, but when the group posts the same ad online, many more people will likely see it than they would in a newspaper or on television.

According to one estimate of media consumption, in 2013, the average US adult spent five hours and sixteen minutes per day viewing online media—about half of that on a phone and half on a desktop or laptop computer. Meanwhile, that same adult spent about four and a half hours watching television. That's a big switch from three years earlier, when the average US adult still spent nearly four and a half hours watching television, but only a little more than three hours online. The biggest loser among media vying for people's attention was newspapers, where the average time spent by adults was just 18 minutes a day in 2013. Facts such as that are one reason interest groups are switching to online communication.

Another big reason for the shift is cost. Sending out information online generally costs less than using print, television, or radio. Marketing has two main costs: the cost to produce the material and the cost to send it out. And the price of producing an ad is about the same, whether it's for television, newspapers, or the Internet. But it costs a lot more to air an ad on television or place it in newspapers than it does to send out the ad via social media or a group's own website. Interest groups still spend money on online advertising—for

People who donate to a campaign are more likely to vote on Election Day. Social media can make it easier for individuals to donate, giving them a stronger voice in the election process.

instance, in an online newspaper—but e-mail and social media allow them to reach more people more quickly for less money. Not only are people more likely to see something online, but it's also much easier for them to share that information with friends.

Some special interest groups and political campaigns are finding a small downside to relying on the Internet. It can be harder for them to reach new audiences and gain new supporters or members. When a group or a campaign runs a television or radio ad, lots of diverse people will see or hear it. But people tend to visit only the websites of groups they already support. Likewise, they tend to follow only the groups they support on social media. And when an organization mails out a brochure or a postcard, that group will probably mail it to everybody in a neighborhood. But if an organization sends an e-mail, it often only has the e-mail addresses of its supporters.

The ability to reach many more people is a great advantage for fund-raising. As Obama's campaign team discovered, candidates can raise a lot of money—and general support— by getting small donations from a lot of people, rather than large donations from just a few people. And with contribution limits in place, one wealthy person or a large group could easily be cut off from donating. A special interest group can have more luck convincing one thousand people to give five dollars each than it can convincing one person to give five thousand dollars. As you may have guessed, social media, text messaging, and e-mail make it even easier to reach those one thousand small-dollar donors.

This grassroots approach to fund-raising can have a big impact on elections. For one thing, it gets more people interested. Once somebody has donated, she or he is more likely to vote on Election Day. Also, with so many more people voicing their opinions through small donations, the wealth of larger special interest groups may become a little less important. Politicians are likely to listen to a big group of voters, even if they don't have the huge money behind them that some special interest groups do. And people on both sides of the political debate agree that getting more people involved is a good thing for US elections.

With the 2016 US presidential election set to be the most expensive in history, there's no doubt election spending will continue to skyrocket. And efforts to reform campaign finance will also continue—both by Congress and state legislatures, as well as in cases decided by the courts. Special interest groups have played a big role in elections for as long as the United States has been a country. That role grew larger than ever in 2010, when the US Supreme Court's decision in *Citizens United v. Federal Election Commission* opened the door for groups to collect and spend unlimited amounts of money—as long as they weren't coordinating with a candidate. Interest groups will continue to play a huge role in elections—but that role will likely keep changing as campaign finance regulations continue to evolve.

# SOURCE NOTES

4 Fredreka Shouten, "Interest Groups Barrage Congress with Sequester Pleas," *USA Today*/Gannett, February 28, 2013, http://www.usatoday.com/story/news/nation/2013/02/28/sequester-lobbying-parks-defense-industry-medical-research/1951327/.

4 Brian Ross, Matthew Mosk, Rhonda Schwartz, and Megan Chuchmach, "Pols, Lobbyists Schmooze at Lavish Convention Parties," *ABC News*, August 12, 2012, http://abcnews.go.com/Blotter/pols-lobbyists-schmooze-lavish-convention-parties/story?id=17099238.

4 Seth Masket, "'Fixing' Campaign Finance Is Only Making It Worse," *Washington Post*, May 12, 2014, http://www.washingtonpost.com/blogs/monkey-cage/wp/2014/05/12/fixing-campaign-finance-is-only-making-it-worse/.

24 Michael Dimino, Bradley Smith, and Michael Solimine, *Voting Rights and Election Law*, New Providence, NJ: Matthew Bender, 2010, https://books.google.com/books?isbn=032717417X.

31 Harry Reid, "Reid Remarks on Constitutional Amendment to Stop Koch Brothers' Unlimited Campaign Spending to Buy Our Democracy," news release, May 15, 2014, http://www.reid.senate.gov/press_releases/2014-05-15-reid-remarks-on-constitutional-amendment-to-stop-koch-brothers-unlimited-campaign-spending-to-buy-our-democracy.

31 Ted Cruz, "Cruz Slams Efforts to Repeal First Amendment," news release, accessed June 3, 2014, http://www.cruz.senate.gov/?p=news&id=1698.

37 Gary Johnson, e-mail to ProCon.org, October 9, 2012, http://2012election.procon.org/view.answers.election.php?questionID=1789.

37 Barack Obama, "Remarks by the President in State of the Union Address," *whitehouse.gov*, January 10, 2010, http://2012election.procon.org/view.answers.election.php?questionID=1789.

41 Gregory J. Krieg, "What Is a Super PAC? A Short History," *ABC News*, August 9, 2012, http://abcnews.go.com/Politics/OTUS/super-pac-short-history/story?id=16960267.

**campaign:** the series of activities organized by a candidate for office, aimed at winning an election

**conservative:** a political movement that favors established, traditional practices in social and political systems

**constituent:** anyone who is a voting member of a community or an organization

**consultant:** a person with a lot of knowledge and experience who gives professional advice to others. Campaign consultants are hired to help candidates win an election.

**convention:** the large meeting where a political party formally chooses the person who will represent the party in an election

**Democrat:** a member of one of the two major political parties in the United States. Democrats tend to favor liberal policies.

**endorse:** to officially support someone in an election campaign

**general election:** the final election to decide which candidate will hold an office. General elections usually follow a primary election.

**liberal:** a political movement that favors reform and broad changes to current social and political systems

**major political party:** a political party that has enough supporters to have major influence in a country's politics. The United States has two major parties: Democratic and Republican.

**nomination:** when a political party officially chooses a candidate to run for election

**ordinance:** a law or a rule made by an authority such as a city government

**primary election:** a first election held to narrow the field of candidates for a general election

**propaganda:** information, often incomplete or biased, that is spread to influence people, especially before an election

**Republican:** a member of one of the two major political parties in the United States. Republicans generally favor conservative policies.

**special interest group:** a group of people that organizes around a shared interest. Special interest groups often lobby to elect candidates who share their interests

Confessore, Nicholas. "Secret Money Fueling a Flood of Political Ads." *New York Times*, October 10, 2014. http://www.nytimes.com/2014/10/11 /us/politics/ads-paid-for-by-secret-money-flood-the-midterm-elections .html?_r=1.

Federal Election Commission. "Public Funding of Presidential Elections (brochure.)" Accessed January 9, 2015. http://www.fec.gov/pages /brochures/pubfund.shtml.

Harvard Kennedy School, Ash Center for Democratic Governance and Innovation: The Transparency Policy Project. "Disclosing Campaign Contributions to Reduce Corruption." Accessed January 9, 2015. http:// www.transparencypolicy.net/campaign-finance.php.

La Raja, Raymond. *Small Change: Money, Political Parties, and Campaign Finance Reform*. Ann Arbor: University of Michigan Press, 2008.

Lunder, Erika K., and L. Paige Whitaker. "501(c)(4) Organizations and Campaign Activity: Analysis under Tax and Campaign Finance Laws." Congressional Research Service 7-5700 (2009). Accessed January 9, 2015. https://www.fas.org/sgp/crs/wmisc/R40183.pdf.

Mutch, Robert E. *Buying the Vote: A History of Campaign Finance Reform*. Oxford: Oxford University Press, 2014.

National Conference of State Legislatures. "Campaign Finance Reform: An Overview." Last modified October 3, 2011. http://www.ncsl.org/research /elections-and-campaigns/campaign-finance-an-overview.aspx.

OpenSecrets.org Center for Responsive Politics. "Types of Advocacy Groups." Accessed January 9, 2015. https://www.opensecrets.org/527s /types.php.

PBS: *Frontline*. "Special Reports: Let the Money Flow." Accessed January 9, 2015. http://www.pbs.org/wgbh/pages/frontline/shows/fixers/reports /letmoney.html.

Public Citizen. "A Short History of the Public Funding of Elections in the US." Last modified July 19, 2012. http://www.citizen.org/documents/short -history-of-public-financing-of-elections.pdf.

"Social Media and Voting." PewResearch. Last modified November 6, 2012. http://www.pewinternet.org/2012/11/06/social-media-and-voting/.

Congress for Kids—Elections
http://www.congressforkids.net/Elections_index.htm
Learn more about candidates, political parties, and elections in this
interactive site just for young people.

Donovan, Sandy. *Media: From News Coverage to Political Advertising.*
Minneapolis: Lerner Publications, 2016.
Read more about how special interest groups and political parties work with
the media to influence elections.

McPherson, Stephanie Sammartino. *Political Parties: From Nominations to
Victory Celebrations.* Minneapolis: Lerner Publications, 2016.
Learn about how political parties move from the nomination to the
election-night results.

Miller, Debra A., ed. *Federal Elections.* Detroit: Greenhaven, 2010.
Learn directly from primary sources in this collection of articles about
elections.

OpenSecrets.org Center for Responsive Politics—Learning Center
https://www.opensecrets.org/resources/learn
Dig deeper into election spending and campaign finance with fact sheets,
timelines, and answers to frequently asked questions on this website from the
Center for Responsive Politics.

Our White House—Race to the Ballot: The *Our White House* Presidential
Campaign and Election Kit for Kids!
http://www.ourwhitehouse.org/campaignandelectionkit.html
Find information, resources, and activities to dig deeper into the topic of
presidential elections.

Expand learning beyond the printed book. Download free, complementary
educational resources for this book from our website, www.lerneresource.com.

## PHOTO ACKNOWLEDGMENTS

The images in this book are used with the permission of: © iStockphoto. com/cajoer, (banners); © iStockphoto.com/jamtoons, (arrows), (stars), (speech bubbles); © iStockphoto.com/ginosphotos, (bunting); © iStockphoto.com/Kontrec, (chalkboard ); © iStockphoto.com/ OliaFedorovsky, (lines); © Pete Souza/The White House/Getty Images, p. 5; © Laura Westlund/Independent Picture Service, p. 7; © John Blanding/The Boston Globe/Getty Images, p. 9; © Bill McCay/WireImage/Getty Images, p. 10; © Pascale Beroujon/Lonely Planet Images/Getty Images, p. 14; © Kalpak Pathak/Hindustan Times/Getty Images, p. 16; © Brian Gomsak/ Getty Images, p. 21; Hector Amezcua/Sacramento Bee/ZUMAPRESS/ Newscom, p. 23; Library of Congress (LC-DIG-ppmsca-35701), p. 24; © Harry Hamburg/NY Daily News Archive/Getty Images, p. 28; ERIK S. LESSER/EPA/Newscom, p. 33; © AF Archive/Alamy, p. 36; © Taylor Hill// WireImage/Getty Images, p. 41; © Thomas Baker/Alamy, p. 44; © Chung Sung-Ju/Getty Images, p. 49; © Jim West/Alamy, p. 53; Courtesy of Barack Obama via Twitter, p. 55; © Chip Somodevilla/Getty Images, p. 57.

Front cover: © iStockphoto.com/Kontrec (chalkboard background); © iStockphoto.com/Electric_Crayon (border); © iStockphoto.com/StasKhom (people and capitol); © iStockphoto.com/cajoer (banners); © iStockphoto. com/OliaFedorovsky (patterns); © iStockphoto.com/jamtoons (doodle arrows).

Back cover: © iStockphoto.com/jamtoons (doodle arrows) (stars).